BEATING THE GATEKEEPERS

BEATING THE GATEKEEPERS

So you can land your next ten jobs

ACME INDUSTRIES

PUT YOUR RESUMES HERE.

H.R. GATEKEEPER

EDWARD H. BURRELL

ACKNOWLEDGMENTS

I would like to recognize my good friend and Christian brother Pat Waggoner whose vast knowledge of the networking process has been a great value to me in formulating a strategy for getting past the gatekeepers. Pat and I have operated a job transition program working to help hundreds of unemployed or underemployed job seekers. The program goals are to equip people with pertinent job hunting information, offer moral support and guide them through the job search process. The program is graciously sponsored by the Crieve Hall Church of Christ in Nashville, Tennessee, where Pat and I are members and where he serves as an elder.

I would like to thank my friend and all-around good guy Lance Finley, principal at Firehouse Design LLC, for his artwork and illustrations. He is super creative and a great collaborator. Working with him has been fun and a lot of laughs.

I would also like to thank my friend, top notch attorney, final proofreader and copy editor Stephanie Kirby for her guidance and encouragement. I would also like to thank Leigh Ray and Jennifer Rudloff, for their proofing and edit work during the early phase of my book.

Finally, I would like to thank my sister Cynthia for her input and guidance. She has been a terrific sounding board, organizer and content editor. I greatly appreciate her help and perspective.

CONTENTS

INTRODUCTION   xi

CHAPTER ONE
Preparations and considerations of a job search   1

The situation   1

The psychology   1

Wrong start   2

Right start   2

Set priorities   3

Steps to begin   4

Define your profession   4

Maintain competitive employability   5

Know your "value-added" equation   5

CHAPTER TWO
Making a plan   7

Objectives and mechanics   7

Priorities and time allocation   8

A concise job plan 8

Activities and considerations 9

Other plan activities to consider 10

Plan for two job searches 11

CHAPTER THREE

Résumé Preparation 13

Write it yourself 13

The most critical part 14

Key components 14

The cover letter 15

Perspective 15

CHAPTER FOUR

The application process 17

The why of job applications 17

A silent disqualification 17

Be prepared 18

Clear, complete and correct form 18

Good references rock and rule 19

"Sync up" your references 20

CHAPTER FIVE

But I have no job experience 21

Getting hired with little or no work experience 21

Skills and attributes 24

No experience can be the least or your problems 25

Test your interview readiness 26

CHAPTER SIX

Living with my choice of college major 29

My degree does not attract employer interest 29

My grades weren't that great either 30

So what subject should I major in? 31

I have experience, but little or no college 32

CHAPTER SEVEN

Defining your employability 35

Recognize how to get a job 35

Learn what employers value 35

Gain a mastery of your profession 36

What to do in a declining industry 37

CHAPTER EIGHT

Grasping the importance of value-added 41

The concept of "value-added" 41

"Value added" in the workplace—professional 42

"Value added" in the workplace—tradesman 44

CHAPTER NINE

Networking 49

Networking activities 49

Be gently persistent 51

How to find networking contacts 52

Employment agencies (a.k.a. head hunters) 53

CHAPTER TEN

The interview process 55

Interview preparations 55
Determine 90 percent of the questions
in advance 56
Four of the most dreaded questions 59
Preparations needed for behavioral interviews 62
Considerations during your interviews 64
Interviewer's considerations 65
Actions behind the interview curtain 65
Job candidates should know 66

CHAPTER ELEVEN

Post interview activities 69

What determines who gets the job offer? 69
Follow-up 70
Don't 71

CHAPTER TWELVE

Summary 73

Job plan strategies 73
Resume tactics 74
Master your profession 74
Know your "value-added equation" 74
Your networking campaign 75
Prepare for the interview 75
Interview performance considerations 76

INTRODUCTION

The scourge of the modern day American job seeker is to submit an application in response to a published job opportunity and never hear back from the company. Behind the scenes, the company receives 400 applications for this same job and someone in the lower echelons of the Human Resources department promptly sorts through them and throws 380 of them away. Within three days, a senior person reviews the 20 still left and throws another 14 away. The remaining six applicants will likely be offered an opportunity to interview for the position. In this book you will learn how to overcome this protocol and get interviews.

I have co-hosted nearly 200 "how to find a job" seminars. After just two sessions, I realized that almost no one is taught what they should do to find employment. Most people know they need a résumé and need to apply for jobs, but beyond those notions they have no experience or proficiency in doing so.

This book is a compilation of best practices I assembled for the job-seeking process working with hundreds of seminar participants and from my role as a senior executive with management responsibilities during the hiring of more than 1,800 people. I know what must be done for you to find employment. My goal with this book is to communicate a job-seeking process that I know will work for you.

Futurists predict that graduating seniors will need 10 jobs before they reach the age of 40. So, it's not all about finding a job. Rather, it's about developing the ability to find your next 10 jobs. Read on to learn how.

During bad economic times, certain workers have an advantage for keeping or landing a job. In this book, you will learn how to become one of the advantaged.

Most job placements are determined as a result of an applicant's performance during the interview. Before you sit down in the interview chair, you should be clear on how you can add value and help a prospective employer. Fortunately, you can determine 90 percent of the likely interview questions in advance. See chapter 10 to learn how you can best find and answer these questions to improve your interview performance.

Special note for those with little or no work experience:

For recent graduates with little or no employment history, this book will teach you what qualities employers are actually looking for in a potential employee. You will learn to evaluate the skills and attributes you possess and phrase them in a way that presents yourself as a qualified candidate in each of your job interviews, whether your resume holds the desired work experience or college major stated in the job listing or not. You will also learn what businesses are all about; important things you need to know and could have learned through work experience. You will gain a significant advantage over other job seekers by learning the "value-added" concept. This understanding will provide you with a powerful tool for improving your interview and networking performance. Finally, you will understand why it is so important to independently research and learn as much about your chosen field as possible.

CHAPTER ONE

Preparations and considerations of a job search

The situation

Most people apply for jobs and never hear anything back. We all need a strategy to get past the front-end gatekeepers who throw our applications and résumés into the trash.

Futurists predict on average a person entering the work force will change jobs 10 times before they reach the age of 40. So, it's not all about finding a job. Rather, it's about developing the ability to find your next 10 jobs.

The psychology

While unemployed and looking for a job, many people experience a profound sense of a lack of control over the process and the outcome. It's easy to become depressed. The process of looking for a job is fraught with rejection, and each kick in the pants is just another reason to feel down. Likewise, being "down in the mouth" is toxic when a person is networking or interviewing.

At some time or another, everyone goes through the indignities of unemployment and must learn to endure the kicks they receive when down. Just know that it is very appealing to a prospective employer to observe a job seeker who can relax, smile and sound upbeat when interviewed.

Make sure you keep a positive attitude; it is an absolutely critical component of your success. Some people actually designate friends to monitor their attitude and to give them feedback periodically on how they are perceived. So, if you are going to feel sorry for yourself, learn to smile during the day and, if necessary, sob in your pillow at night.

The truth is that one can exercise a great deal of control when seeking employment by engaging in activities and processes that will lead to a job. If you prepare and go through the proper motions, you will find a job. Process is the most important part and you can control it.

Wrong start

Many people start their job seeking efforts with a burst of activities. They rush out to get fancy paper, print up a bunch of slick résumés and attempt to market themselves with even slicker cover letters. For their electronic version, they jazz up the fonts and graphics, then they add boxes, colors and underlining until the resume looks like a Christmas tree. Once satisfied, they fire their resume at anything that moves. If they hear nothing back, they frantically repeat the process. If still no response, they feverishly seek help in making their resume package fancier and flashier.

Right Start

The process that will lead to a successful job search requires a preparation phase to make sure the product (you) is ready to go to market. The process of finding employment begins with you concluding and declaring what your profession or occupation is and by achieving mastery in talking about it. This is important because networking is king. Networking effectively will put you in control of the process and get responses to your resume submissions. But, to network before you are ready to represent your profession competently is likely to hurt your efforts rather than help.

The damage would be even worse if you were to interview before you are ready. You do that and you can kiss a position with that company good-bye, as it is difficult to overcome a poor first impression, especially when made during an interview.

You should know that being good at your profession has profoundly less value if you can't communicate your abilities proficiently. In fact, this can work against you in a dramatic way if your talk doesn't match the expectations created by your résumé. For example, if you have 10 years of technical experience listed on your resume, but you express your thoughts like you have two years of experience, the interviewer's assessment of your capabilities will be very negative.

Set priorities

Finding the right job is all about making its pursuit the highest priority in your life. Now turn off the television and make a resolution not to turn it back on until you have a job. You must get up early every day and work at job-hunting activities. While it is a good thing to spend time with your friends and family, it is essential that you separate work time from leisure time. You certainly could squeeze in some television, but you would be far better off using all your energy to research the Internet for things that may speed up the job search process. The Internet is a great resource to find news about companies in your line of work and to research business-related information you receive while networking.

Illustration J-1.1 © *Edward H. Burrell*

Turn off the television until you find a job.

Steps to begin

- Determine what you want to be when you grow up, regardless of your age.
- Maintain competitive employability.
- Know your "value-added" equation.

Define your profession

Clearly defining your profession is an essential first step. You've got to be clear about what you are before you can practice talking about it. This is necessary so you can talk professionally and effectively while you're networking or interviewing.

Maintain competitive employability

In addition to studying, defining and analyzing all you've done in the work place, it is essential to increase your occupational reading and continuously work to build your computer skills. Make it a habit to turn off the television and spend your time accumulating information and building skills related to your profession. Read about the latest techniques that have worked well for others and those that haven't. You can search the Internet for tutorials and videos to learn how to do just about anything on earth. So take advantage of this immense body of knowledge, most of which is available to you for free.

Know your "value-added" equation

There is good news for high performers during economic downturns. When things are tight, businesses quickly realize the need to hire and maintain a highly productive workforce. As a consequence, companies are always looking to trade up and rid themselves of lower performers in favor of the best performers. You want to be classified as a high performer. You do that by understanding what actions add value to your company and then figure out how you can provide that value. In any business, both the employer and employees should have an understanding, based on hard numbers, of what adds value.

If you are employed by a business, large or small, you can understand "value-added" better if you ask, and honestly answer, these questions:

- How does this company or my boss make money, and what role do I play in the process?
- Do I understand how the functions of my job benefit the company and bring monetary value for our customers?

If you are going into business for yourself, you must fully understand the principle of "value-added." You should also do your best to make sure your employees understand it well enough to see how it works in the course of their daily work. If you work for someone else, you should do your best to thoroughly understand how your work makes profit for your boss. This understanding will help you land the next job, perform better in your current job and enable you to negotiate a better salary when salary and benefit questions arise. You will find out more about this in the pages that follow.

CHAPTER TWO

Making a plan

Objectives and mechanics

Before a plan can be assembled, you must decide exactly what you are trying to accomplish. Once this is determined it is necessary to evaluate and determine what activities are necessary to bring about the accomplishment of the desired result, also known as an objective. What does a job-seeker's objective look like? Only you can decide your objective, but let's assume you want a job with career growth potential located within certain geographical boundaries. You require a specific level of pay and would like to be with a competitive company in an industry that will be around for a long time. With that simple statement, you've got yourself a good job seeker's objective.

The purpose of a plan is to provide organization, sequencing, timelines and frequency to a set of activities. The plan will then provide a guide for the accomplishment of the person's goals or objectives. The plan itself doesn't accomplish objectives, but it serves as a blueprint to be followed to that end. The implementation of the plan by its author is what leads to the accomplishment of the objectives.

Priorities and time allocation

It is important to select the right activities and allocate time to them in accordance with their value. You will not find a job sitting at home. The majority of job seekers consistently credit networking as the number one source of new jobs. Therefore, you should spend most of your time preparing for or participating in networking activities.

To make this point, many job seekers have come to our job seminars extremely frustrated. They made application to hundreds of jobs through Internet websites, but never got an interview. Most never even heard back from anyone, other than countless scammers trying to sign them up to buy or sell products. In most cases this was the only real job seeking activity these people engaged in. Here's the problem: less than 10 percent of job seekers identify online job sites as the source that led to their employment. Thus, applying to jobs online should not be the most utilized action in your job plan, but rather should make up less than 10 percent of your planned activities. Correspondingly, networking activities have been identified as the most productive source of people finding jobs, so they should make up the majority of your planned activities.

A concise job plan

Below I have illustrated an example of an extremely concise job seeker's plan to make a point; don't lose sight of what's important about a job plan. The two items listed in my plan are the focal points. You will have many other plan activities, but they all should be action items in support of your development as a candidate and activities related to your job search.

1. Within the next 21 days, prepare yourself to achieve, exhibit and communicate a mastery of your profession at the degree necessary to land a job.

2. When preparations are complete, get in front of people in your desired industry and targeted companies. Repeat the process until you get a job offer.

Activities and considerations

Make a plan for your job-search activities and follow your plan. Start every day with three to five objectives that you must get accomplished that day. A key recurring objective should be to make face-to-face contact with five to eight people working in companies associated with your industry every day. The weekly plan should include at least 50 hours of activities. These activities should include: perfecting a scripted discussion about the functions of your profession, researching the Internet for knowledge, attending business or industry events, and participating in lunches or meetings with people in your industry. You must also spend time on a recurring basis building and maintaining your professional skills.

Business people are busy. Once you are out of sight for 10 minutes, you are out of mind as well. After you've pulled out of the parking lot, even your best network contacts have moved on to their job activities of the day and have long since forgotten you. Make sure your plan is designed to overcome this circumstance. For example, to help avoid this outcome, you should plan to continuously follow up with your contacts. You must find a comfortable rhythm and approach to put your shining face in front of these people without alienating them or having them file a restraining order against you. One day, they might need you, and when they see you, they will remember you and you may be offered an opportunity with them or someone in their business network.

Other plan activities to consider

- Consult with job seekers at job program events.
- Schedule informational interviews with your network contacts. Ask questions then listen.
- Establish communication with employers through personal contact.
- Learn how to present yourself professionally to employers.
- Develop a target list of employers and learn about them.
- Constantly work to improve your interviewing skills.
- Find places that help job seekers.
- Set aside time for continuous job education and skill improvement.
- Establish a schedule for recurring contact with:
  - o Your key network contacts
  - o Job assistance programs
  - o State employment offices
  - o Professional organizations
  - o Industry contacts
  - o Employment agencies
  - o Employer websites (check for job availabilities)
  - o Targeted employers
- Conduct brainstorming sessions with friends and other job seekers.
- Set up a process to track your job application submissions and keep a record of what you sent including your résumé, cover letter and any other materials.
- Keep a record of the contacts you make. Include the company name, names of individuals, dates and details of the contact.
- Establish a job activities calendar to manage your meetings, events and follow up schedule.

- Develop résumés for the industries you're targeting.
- Make a list of people you know, would like to know.
- Find organizations that sponsor networking events or job help activities.
- Find and bookmark helpful websites and those of your targeted companies.
- Identify the relevant professional associations for your field.
- Search for job-related salary information on the Internet.

Plan for two job searches

It's quite likely your target job will take some time to find, so it is a good idea to find a temporary job to help pay the bills. Include in your plan the activities needed to find a plan B job as a placeholder. It is better to have any job than to be unemployed. Having a job tends to make us feel more positive and perform better when networking and interviewing.

CHAPTER THREE

Résumé preparation

Write it yourself

Many people think a résumé written by some résumé guru will be the ticket to getting them a job. While it is true that a well written résumé is necessary and very helpful, there is no guarantee that the guru you select will write a good one. Even if you chose your guru wisely, the writer is still stuck with telling the story of your job history. If your job history is poorly conveyed to them or marginal in its own right, at best you will have a well written narrative detailing a marginal job history. Or even worse, the writer waxes poetic and writes a fairy tale. Then, when you are called upon to represent yourself in an interview, it will be obvious that you didn't write your résumé, it isn't truthful, or both.

There is intrinsic value to be gained from writing your own résumé. First, you will avoid the loss-of-face that comes with your interviewer knowing you didn't write your own résumé. Secondly, and equally important, is the benefit that you derive when you are forced to think in depth about the activities and issues in your employment history. This working knowledge of your job history will be a significant aid to you when you interview. Finally, professional résumé writers can be very expensive and you must be a good steward of your financial resources because you will incur many other job search expenses to come. My suggestion is that you write your own résumé but solicit help from a guru or someone with proficiency in writing to give you feedback.

If you haven't created or revised your résumé in a while, it's no big deal. Just find a good example on the Internet to use as a formatting guide. You will have to dig up the dates of your previous employment and various other facts and figures. These tasks can be time consuming, but you only have to do them once.

The most critical part

While résumés are seen in many formats, the key thing to know is the top half of the first page is the most critical. In many cases, it may be the only thing read and its content will determine if your résumé is moved on in the process or thrown in the reject pile. So the priority here is to be certain you articulate your noteworthy experience and significant accomplishments on that precious few square inches of paper.

Key components

The key résumé components are the *heading* with your contact information followed by a *summary paragraph* of your noteworthy experience and major accomplishments. Next, list your *job experience* starting with your most recent job and continue back to your first job. For each job, identify the company name and location, the dates of employment and your job title. Then, identify your duties and responsibilities. When describing your prior job responsibilities, be sure to explain your significant accomplishments. In all cases, after you describe the job, you should explain what you did, the contributions you made, and, more specifically, how you moved the needle and made things better. If you can't think of anything special that you contributed, you now know how important it is to have a constructive story to tell. In your next job, you should strive to add value in your workplace, improve the process, make a difference and give yourself something to brag about the next time you are looking for a job. *The final section of your résumé is for your education, certifications, language proficiencies and any other unique qualifications you may have.*

The cover letter

When you send your résumé to a potential employer, you should include a letter of introduction and explanation. This letter is commonly referred to as a cover letter. The cover letter in its simplest form is meant to inform the employer who you are, what position you are applying for and how to contact you. Many people suggest you use the cover letter as an opportunity to sell yourself. If you choose to do so, keep it brief and make a strong connection between your abilities and their needs. Use specific examples of what you have accomplished in a similar environment, but keep it at a high level and don't simply repeat what is on your résumé. Be specific on how your skills and experience match the job description and qualifications of the job for which you are applying. Find a well-written cover letter example on the Internet and decide your best approach.

Perspective

It may surprise some that this chapter is relatively short because they believe a résumé to be the most important preparation for their job search. Once they have one in hand, they think their job search preparation is mostly done. The reality is just the opposite, a completed résumé only serves to kick off the job search process. A résumé is a bit like a concert ticket, you must have one to gain entrance to the event. Unlike a concert where the tickets are sold to anyone, first come, first served, résumés are selected for interviews by employers for very specific reasons. A concert ticket allows the holder admission and includes a seat assignment. In the hiring process, determining who gets a chance for a seat merely begins with the selection of résumés. Once a résumé is selected, it becomes a simple administrative placeholder. It does nothing but hold a place in line for you until you are invited to give an oral representation of your résumé to a prospective employer by answering his or her questions at the interview.

By the end of the interview process, the résumé is completely forgotten and the focus turns exclusively to how well you represented your experience, skills, attributes and potential during the interview. It is your performance during the interview that will win you a job offer and not your résumé. Yes, you must have a reasonably good résumé, but that should be done in a couple of days. You need to simply get it done so that you can begin the more time consuming aspects of the job search preparation process. This book is a compilation of how you conquer the rest of the process.

CHAPTER FOUR

The application process

The why of job applications

There is good reason why companies require everyone to complete their application form—even if they already have a copy of the person's résumé. The company needs to perform checks and validations required as part of their hiring process. Things like background checks, employment history validations, education verifications and possibly credit checks are all part of the process. Some of these checks may require the person's consent before the prospective employer can request them. That's one reason they require you to sign your application. The other reason is to have you certify the information is correct.

A silent disqualification

Applications are frequently filled out hurriedly; as a consequence people are often stumped and can't remember the details of the required information. Some will just "wing it," and put down in cryptic notes the best they can remember. Unfortunately for them, the company will attempt to verify many if not all of their representations and when they do, they fail. They fail because the information provided is illegible, incomplete or just wrong. At that point, you will be disqualified and taken out of the running for the position you seek. Most likely that will happen behind the scenes and you will never know why. At best, they may set your application aside with the intent to follow up with you for whatever further information they need. This creates a risk for you to fall by the wayside and be forgotten.

Be prepared

In my experience as an employer, we often got to the interview phase with job candidates and on short notice asked them to fill out our corporate application form just prior to their interview. This can be a nightmare for anyone not prepared with the necessary information. If you do not have the job application data figured out and written down, you will be inconvenienced and slowed down. You may have to go back to the company with information or mail it back. All of this is wasted motion and presents an opportunity to have some of your paperwork lost or misplaced. Gathering this information is a pain, but you will have to do it eventually. If you wait until you need it, you will find it very inconvenient and damaging to your job-seeking efforts.

The moral of this story is: Nothing good can come from being unprepared to fill out job applications. In fact, you can lose a job opportunity when your data fails verification efforts. So you should take the job application seriously and make every effort to make it as easy as possible for potential employers to verify your job application data.

Clear, complete and correct form

The good news is that there is commonality in the application data required by employers. Below I have listed the usual suspects that show up on employment applications that require data. Write clearly and neatly using a standard blue or black ink pen. Spell out words and write in complete sentences. Review your application for spelling and grammar. Don't leave any blanks.

- Employment history: Name of employer with address and contact information, position held, salary, duties and responsibilities, dates of employment, supervisor and reason for leaving. The number of past employers required will likely cover up to the last 10 years.
- Have you ever been convicted of a criminal offense (felony or misdemeanor)? Yes or no. If yes, provide details.
- Education: Name and address of school, college or institution, major, degrees or certifications earned and date of graduation.
- References: Have at least three, either personal or professional. People you have worked for are best. Be prepared with names, job title or relationship, addresses and phone numbers.
- Employment eligibility: Over 18, citizen or appropriate authorization and date of your availability to start work.
- Skills and Qualifications: licenses, skills, training, awards
- Military service: Branch of service, rank, dates of service, skills and type of discharge.
- Your signature certifying the data.

Good references rock and rule

Past employer references are very important. Not all the references you list on your application will be contacted by every prospective employer. When they are, what your references say to a prospective employer will likely determine whether or not you are offered the job. Why? Because hiring the right person is always important and many times critical. People making hiring decisions do not want to make a mistake. The mere fact that they are calling your references suggests they are looking for confirmation of what they thought they saw in you. Often times they have formulated an opinion, but having that opinion validated by the person's previous employer/supervisor is very powerful. You make your best impressions during the interview when you talk about what you did and how well you did it. Having your previous employer echo your accomplishments is the "mother lode" of references. This kind of alignment can happen spontaneously, but since many people do not remember what they had for lunch yesterday, it is unlikely your previous boss will remember the specifics of what you did on the job two or three years ago. In my next paragraph, I describe how you can take the initiative and help them remember. If you take this action, your good interview impression can be reinforced by an even better impression given by your previous employers.

"Sync up" your references

Make a list of people you have worked under as potential employment references. Locate them and discuss their willingness to provide an employment reference for you. If they agree, ask for current contact information. Work up a fact sheet relevant to each individual reference and provide it to them along with an updated résumé. The fact sheet should include information and circumstances pertaining to your previous work relationship with them. Include your important accomplishments and/or the job history you hope to get visibility with your potential new employer. This reminder will help your references better remember you and represent you more effectively when your potential employer calls them for a recommendation. You want your stories to sync up. Not that you are making stuff up, but you want to refresh the memory of your references and lead them to accurately recall the key issues that are important for them to convey to your prospective employer.

CHAPTER FIVE

But I have no job experience

Getting hired with little or no work experience

I want to debunk the number one mistaken belief I see among young people with little or no experience. That mistaken belief is that they can't compete for jobs because they don't have the required experience. Of the hundred or so young people I have interviewed, my guess is less than 10 percent engaged in serious interview preparations. More than half of the hundred seemingly made no effort to prepare at all; they sat there answering questions and just made stuff up as we went along. I could tell others had made some effort to research my company on the internet because they had a few manufactured questions they dutifully asked of me at the end of the interview. The truth is most of the rejection young people encounter in their job search is a consequence of a lack of preparation and a corresponding inability to present their capabilities effectively and not because of their work history.

Yes, if you submit your resume in response to a job opportunity and you don't meet the work experience requirements, 99 out of 100 times you will not hear back. We all face experience hurdles at some time or another, even those with many years of experience. If the hiring authority does not think a person's experience is applicable, it's like it doesn't exist. There are also instances where a hiring manager has it in their head a certain work history is necessary for someone to be prepared for their position. It doesn't matter if that experience really isn't necessary, they believe it is and they control the hiring decision. These situations and variations thereof do exist, but they only represent one slice of the job market. Most opportunities do not require people to have such a tightly defined experience history. Don't dwell on the negative rather move on to those jobs where you can win an interview.

For the jobs that require in-depth knowledge or specific experience, you simply will not be considered if you lack that experience. On the other hand, there are many jobs that require little to no experience. In these positions, individuals either learn as they go (on-the-job training) or the job provides its own job specific training program. In between these two extremes you will find a broad range of job experience requirements. It is within this range where you can often posture your skills and attributes to demonstrate value equal to or greater than the applicable experience requirements. Often it will require you to network your way to an interview because your resume includes little or no experience, but networking is what we all need to do to get past the gatekeepers anyway.

Most applicants don't hear back when they submit their resume in response to a job posting, but the reasons vary a great deal. That's why I wrote this book and named it "Beating the Gatekeepers". The company probably received 400+ applications and yours was an easy throw away—because at face value you didn't meet the experience requirements and they didn't know you so boom in the trash went your application. The solution to this is the same for everyone; you must prepare narratives that demonstrate your qualities, skills and attributes (whether you possess enough work experience or not). You must learn about the target job so you can explain how your capabilities can be relevant to its functions and are a reasonable substitute for its experience requirement. With that understanding, you must practice talking these narratives through until you have achieved a polished and relaxed manner.

To be clear, when I ask that you prepare narratives to explain your capabilities, this is not a situation where you make a perfectly rehearsed long and tedious speech about your skills and positive attributes. Rather, you must be prepared to sit in the interview and skillfully answer a steady stream of questions. It is in the formulation of your answers, in the quality of your communication and in the veracity of the how, what and why of your responses where you will display your capabilities. So your interview preparations should include practice formulating answers to a range of likely questions related to your targeted job. You will read more about answering interview questions later in this book.

I don't want to minimize the value of work experience, because experience is important. Equally, if not more important however, are the skills, attributes and attitude the individual conveys during the interview process. Said another way, an individual could have two years of experience selling cars, but not actually have succeeded in selling any. The ingredients to the secret sauce an employer is searching for in a candidate are most often a person's attitude, communication ability and willingness to work hard. These are not qualities you gain from experience; you either have them or you don't. These attributes can help to overcome many shortcomings such as a lack of work experience (just in case you don't have those two years of mediocre sales results). Okay, so I can be a little sarcastic, but I want you to get the point.

Here is what this scenario looks like in real life. If I am the prospective employer and I have two candidates in front of me: One candidate who has two years of experience selling cars, but has a record of mediocre results. The second candidate appears to have high energy, a great attitude and good communication skills, but no actual selling experience. Do I want to settle for a poor salesman and spend time trying to energize them or do I want to hire the individual with high potential and teach them some sales techniques? In my experience with hundreds of hiring actions, high potential wins most of the time. Be aware that not every interviewer automatically thinks this way. Hiring managers often think of skills and attributes as synonymous with people that have the benefit of a certain work history. You have to win them over with words that portray your skills and attributes in a way that connects them to the target job. Take the opportunity and explain what you can do to be a success, you have nothing to lose.

Skills and attributes

For clarification purposes, what I mean by skills and attributes is:

> Skills = abilities, talents, expertise and proficiencies.
> Attributes = qualities, characteristics and traits.

Skills can substitute for work experience, but only if you present them well in your interviews. Listed below are several skills that are customarily recognized as necessary and valuable in the workplace:

- General computer capabilities
- Proficiency with Microsoft Word and Excel
- Business math skills
- Strong written and verbal communication skills

- Team skills
- Leadership skills
- Critical thinking skills- the ability to analyze and anticipate situations, define problems and recognize solutions

Even if you have experience, it helps to have an education related to the job you seek. So if you still have some high school or college ahead of you, be very thoughtful about your course selection. Be sure to select classes that have relevance and will enhance your skill set for job opportunities that motivate you.

Attributes complete the package. An employer can teach you how to do almost anything, but they can't teach you innate characteristics such as: a strong work ethic, loyalty, reliability, personal accountability, or a positive attitude. You have to bring these qualities with you. For your interview, you must have narratives prepared that help you show off your desirable attributes.

Time and again hiring managers can't find people with the specific experience they want, so they look to candidates they think have the best potential. That's where you can shine and ultimately win the job by making a persuasive presentation of your skills and attributes. When you do, you will demonstrate the capabilities a prospective employer is looking for and they will see you as the perfect candidate for the job. In other words, when properly presented, your lack of experience can be eclipsed by your attributes and skills.

No experience can be the least of your problems

The truth is people have been entering the workforce for hundreds of years without work experience. Most large companies have recruiting programs specifically targeted at recent graduates or people who are starting out at entry level.

If you have little or no experience and a company chooses

to interview you anyway; you have a real shot at the job. If they don't select you for the position after the interview, it was not for your lack of experience. Just on the face of it you know that reason can't be true in most if not every situation. It's not true because the company had your application and resume. They knew your work history before they brought you in. No company conducts interviews with people they deem unqualified. It costs too much money and it takes too much time. If you didn't get offered the job it was because your interview performance was not as convincing as it needed to be. This is true even if they say you aren't qualified because of a lack of experience. This is a nice way of letting you down rather than saying they don't like what they saw during your interview. If you walk away from a poor interview performance letting yourself off the hook by accepting the wrong reason for your rejection, then you have no hope of identifying the issues you need to improve on. Just remember, the job is won or lost based on the success of your interview. A good interview performance requires diligence and preparation. A well performed interview can overcome a gap in experience and almost any other shortcomings.

Because there are many factors besides experience that contribute to an individual's capacity to do a job well, it is essential that you stop making a lack of work experience such a big deal in your own mind. If you have doubts about your qualifications, your self-doubt will adversely affect your ability to sell yourself during your interviews.

Test your interview readiness

Okay, so you don't have much if any job experience, but you've got skills and attributes, right? Here is a good test question to help you determine if you are ready for an interview. Assume you got the job, now ask yourself one question: do I know what I would do on Monday when I start work? Whoops, you don't have a good answer for that? Experience or not, you must understand how you can add value to the company before you sit down in the interview chair and that starts with knowing what you will do when you show up to work. The value-added concept is explored further later in this book. Without experience at that job, how do you know what you would do on Monday? First, you read and study about the job. Then ask questions of people who do know what you should do to get an even better perspective. Knowing the fundamentals of the job will boost your confidence and your interview preparation will make an otherwise mundane performance exceptional and compelling.

CHAPTER SIX

Living with my choice of college major

My degree does not attract employer interest

I have some good news and some bad news. While most professional positions require a college degree, many do not require a specific degree. Companies will regularly state a degree preference, but often do not prohibit others from applying and competing for the job. The bad news is there are many degrees that employers don't seem to value in job applicants. If, for example, you have a BS in history, and the position requires analytical capabilities, the interviewer will likely not be impressed. In many cases this could be a deal breaker, so it is up to you to convince them that you have skills and attributes that more than compensate for any perceived educational deficiencies.

One good remedy for a degree that gets no traction in the job market is to sign up with employment agencies and target your assignments toward companies in industries that would be excellent places to work. It may be necessary to take temporary assignments in lesser capacity jobs to get your foot in the door of these companies. Here's where the good news comes in, once you're in a company, the focus totally turns to your performance. If you are a high performer, no one cares what your college major was. So even though you had to start out at a lower than optimum job level, you will be in a good industry and have significant upward mobility.

The really good news I bring is from my observations during several years working in the corporate world; there are many people without the sought-after majors that do exceedingly well in moving up the corporate food chain. Mostly they are top notch performers who are also first-rate communicators, both verbal and written. If you communicate skillfully people automatically think you are smart and capable.

My grades weren't that great either

If you are a recent graduate with little or no work experience, your prospective employers will give serious consideration to your grade point average. If your grades were good, you will start your interview in a positive light. You still must present yourself well, but you are off to a good start. If your grades are marginal or poor, and you are still lucky enough to get an interview, you can bet your interviewer will be thinking about your poor grades and will likely ask you questions as to why you performed so poorly. The best answer I have ever heard, and frankly won me over, was where a young man came straight out and said all the things he did wrong away from home in his first couple of years in college. He explained that if I reviewed his grade point for his junior and senior years, I would see he had done considerably better. I did and he had. You may have a similar story to tell. Think through your situation and circumstances and prepare a truthful, yet judicious explanation because you will need one.

Remember, presenting your skills or attributes well can substitute for a lack of work experience. They can likewise make up for a weak college major or a poor academic performance. I'm not going to sugarcoat this, with a poor academic record you have dug a hole and you will need to work extra hard to prepare a powerful representation of your capabilities and their relevance to the target job.

So what subject should I major in?

Unfortunately, college majors in History, Psychology, Criminal Justice, Political Science, Drama, Fine Arts, Anthropology, Archeology, English Literature, Philosophy and most other arts and humanities subjects are not readily identifiable to any industry. If you choose one of these majors, many employers in the corporate world will have a hard time seeing how your educational background connects to their business.

Before I identify what I see as the most employable college major, I want to say there are many great subjects to choose from. For example, if you have chosen to be an engineer, an accountant or a nurse, your major is chosen for you. A big part of choosing a major will be dependent upon the individual's strengths and interests. Any major like these that has a recognizable career association and where an individual holds passion would likely serve them well.

My answer is oriented toward business. I choose business because in my experience, a degree in business never seemed to disqualify many, if any, job applicants. I also know a degree in business relates to a huge segment of the employment sector. I have a BS in accounting. I majored in accounting because I wanted to be successful in business, not to be an accountant. While it has been critical for me to understand revenue and expenses, financial analysis and cost accounting, there are a few other skills/disciplines that have been extremely important as well. Statistics and quantitative measures have been a dominant force in my business life. The same is true for my understanding of computers and computer systems. I took just one course in computer programming which included a section on the basic components and mechanics of computer systems. That course provided me with a terrific platform to understand technology in general. Other very important elements in my education included courses in public speaking and written communications. Finally, I needed strong business math skills.

As it turned out, all of these disciplines fit neatly in my business-oriented curriculum. In short, I think a degree in business has the broadest application and is a safe and flexible choice. I would strive to take the business degree courses that teach the skills I mentioned in chapter five and the core subjects I discussed in the paragraph above.

When employers select a candidate, actual experience or a certain college degree is only a part of the decision process. The bigger part is finding the person with the right skills and attributes. So those of you who are worried about your lack of work experience or less marketable college degree now have a path to becoming more competitive in the job market. Learn how to persuasively give emphasis to your skills and attributes and demonstrate how they apply to a targeted job. Do this well and you will win the job.

I have experience, but little or no college

From my perspective, this is a much more difficult circumstance to contend with than that of the college graduate with no experience. As I mentioned before, once you are employed no one cares what your college major was. That observation does apply here as well, but there is one wrinkle. To advance in many professional jobs you have to be a college graduate. I have seen people move up the corporate food chain without a college degree, but they are few and far between and it is a tough road to travel. Worst of all, it is especially hard to find a replacement job if you leave the company where you have worked your way up into the professional ranks.

Having said that, your attributes and skills can help you in this circumstance much the same as in the scenarios I described earlier. I would add one more piece of advice. Unless you are working toward a college degree, whatever self-improvement time you spend should first be spent working to improve your verbal and written communication skills. I know the return on that investment is profound.

CHAPTER SEVEN

Defining your employability

Recognize how to get a job

The simple answer: Get an interview and do well in the interview.

You are likely to need to do well in three to five different job interviews to get one job offer.

How do I get an interview? Answer: Get up early, get out of the house and plan a schedule that puts you face to face with five to eight people related to your industry every day.

How do I do well in the interview? Answer: Study the functions of the job or your profession and practice talking about them. Identify in advance the questions you will face during your interview and practice answering them. You can identify 90 percent of the questions in advance of the interview. The techniques for doing so follow in a few pages.

Learn what employers value

Do you fully understand how your work adds value to the company and brings monetary value to its customers? How does this company make money, and what role do you play in the process? Your potential new boss will be pondering these two questions: Can this person make me money and can this person save me money? Before you sit down in the interview chair, you should be clear on how you can help a prospective employer.

The value-added concept is essential to all businesses, even nonprofits, such as charity hospitals, museums and other institutions. If a nonprofit doesn't provide value to its community, after a while the community will cut funding. If the situation persists, the nonprofit will wither and die.

"Value-added" applies to every work environment. If you are to be successful, then your employer must feel they are getting what they need, and a little bit more. When you apply for a job, make sure your prospective employer sees the value-added component in you. Even more important: Once you have the job, keep your value-added promise by doing your job well and satisfying the customers. If you do those things, you will stand a much better chance of getting the job, doing it well and earning promotions.

Gain a mastery of your profession

It is important to analyze your job or profession through to its component activities. Think about situations that commonly occur in this job environment. Now, think through the best way to accomplish each of these activities. Recount all the tasks required in a detailed written outline. Create a two-minute discussion on each function or step that makes up your job, and practice talking about it. You should be able to identify and recite things that commonly go wrong, and what must be done to accomplish these functions, even under difficult situations. Be ready to give examples of how you were able to overcome obstacles and accomplish the tasks. Also, distinguish between the right way and the wrong way of getting things done. Continuously read, analyze, talk and improve your written outline. As you do, you will discover important details that will significantly strengthen your narratives. Your narratives will be a work in progress as you constantly talk and sharpen them during your networking interactions.

Once you have perfected your script and can communicate a solid grasp of your profession, you appear to others as a high-quality professional. This will motivate the people you meet while networking to refer you to their business contacts. They will do it to help their business associates, as opposed to simply helping you. You still benefit from the referral, but their true motivation will be to help their business network because they believe in you. This type of motivation adds enormous power to their referral and will help you get jobs whether you are mowing lawns or performing brain surgery.

Always be prepared to represent your professional capabilities, as you never know when you may find yourself in a networking moment. Many business people are constantly trolling for talent and you want to present yourself as a serious professional any time you have an audience. If you are prepared, your networking will get you interviews, and your performance during your interviews will get you job offers.

What to do in a declining industry

Many people come from industries that have downsized or disappeared. While some battered industries might come back, their recovery may be too far in the future to help you. Don't get stuck in a fading industry. An old adage says that doing the same thing and expecting a different result is one definition of insanity. Adapt to new truths. If you are in a declining industry, separate yourself from that industry by stripping away all the technical terms, acronyms and industry-specific products associated with your last job, and redefine yourself by concentrating on the skills you have mastered that are easily transferable to the job you want. While certainly not in a declining industry, my brothers and sisters leaving the military would benefit from these tactics as well. When I created my experience narratives after my Army service, I left out all the military terminology and listed my job skills, abilities and functions in their purest form.

In essence, companies are looking to evaluate how your education, skills, knowledge, behaviors and experience match up with the job description for which they are recruiting. Most of these attributes are not industry specific or do not have to be industry specific. So by separating yourself from your defunct industry, you will have a whole new world of opportunities to pursue.

When writing your résumé or your job function outline, concentrate on your skills, knowledge, behavior, personal qualities and experience without connecting it to the military or your defunct industry.

- Skills: These fall in two categories, transferable skills or all other skills. First, focus on your transferable skills— those basic skills you use to do everything else—such as reading, writing, math, speaking and listening skills. Then, focus on all your other skills, such as decision-making skills, interpersonal skills, financial skills, analytical skills, resource management skills, technology skills, etc.
- Knowledge: It is different for everybody, so just simply address the knowledge you have that is specific to the job you seek.
- Behaviors and personal qualities, also known as attributes: These include words that describe your work ethic and can be applicable to any industry: cooperative, punctual, loyal, determined, focused, mature, open-minded, flexible, embraces change, positive, work-oriented, etc. Be bold in your narratives and illustrations, and talk about them without a connection to a specific industry.

- Experience: Keep it in perspective to the functions of the specific job you seek and stay away from an industry context.

Be ready to cite examples of your skills, knowledge, attributes and experience showing how they apply to any job. Be sure to formulate your answers using your accomplishments as examples of what you did and will do in future actions.

Once you have freed yourself from a specific industry and you change your focus to industries that are hiring, you will discover there are companies and industries that you never knew existed. You will find out about them through a determined networking effort. To be clear: there is nothing wrong with seeking a job similar to your last one; it is only bad when you exclude other possibilities. This is especially true if your industry is in the tank.

Illustration J-1.2 © *Edward H. Burrell*

Redefine yourself so you can focus on industries that are hiring.

CHAPTER EIGHT

_____

Grasping the importance of value-added

The concept of "value-added"

The first rule of any job is: You must produce. What does that mean? It means different things in different jobs. If you are a brick mason, you have to build walls and other structures. If you are a nurse, you must give your patients proper care. If you are a car salesman, you must sell cars. In a competitive marketplace, you must perform these tasks at a competitive cost and well enough that someone is willing to pay your salary or buy your services. In addition, it is important that you perform your duties better than the average member of your peer group. In most occupations, if you are not working efficiently and effectively, you will soon be out of a job and you will find it difficult to get another one. This is true because companies do not want to hire inefficient and ineffective employees. As simple as this concept sounds, many people do not understand what it looks like in the workplace. *Just remember someone somewhere in management is comparing the cost of your employment versus the value of your output.*

"Value-added" is the notion that an employee should earn his or her company the amount the employee is being paid, plus additional money to help cover the cost of doing business (a portion of everything from rent for an office to gas for the company car), plus something more. The "something more" is profit. Profits add value to a business, and that is the employer's ultimate goal when hiring any employee.

"Value-added" in the workplace—professional

Law firms provide an excellent example of the value-added concept. Let's look at how it works for an attorney in a fairly large firm. The firm pays him an annual salary, and for his salary, he is expected to earn his pay by performing the legal chores the firm's clients need. This takes time, which is recorded in the form of billable hours—hours for which the clients pay. His work must satisfy the needs of these clients. That way they keep paying for the service and may even refer other clients to the firm. The firm provides the attorney with an office. The firm has a staff, meeting rooms, office equipment and various other costs associated with operating the firm's business. If the attorney wants things to go well between his firm and himself, he must generate more billable hours (more income) than it costs the firm to pay his salary and his share of those other expenses. If he does this, both he and his firm should prosper. The money clients pay over and above his salary and expenses is *value-added*. By generating more revenue than it costs to keep him working, the attorney has added real value to his firm.

If the attorney doesn't do a good job or bills clients too many hours to get a job done, the clients will become unhappy with his services, and then they will go elsewhere for their legal needs. As this happens, the firm is still paying his salary and the other expenses associated with him working there. That means he is costing the firm more money than he is bringing in, and is, therefore, losing the firm's money. If this continues, the company eventually shows him the door.

Luckily, the attorney in my example is an efficient and productive lawyer. His billable hours average 10 percent more than his peers and not only pay his salary but also pay the freight on his office, his part of staff expenses and a share of all the other costs related to the law firm's business. His billable hours generate enough so that when all of those expenses are added up, and the total is subtracted from the amount the attorney brings in, there's something left. That's profit, which is the basis of what he adds to the overall value of the firm.

If our intrepid lawyer loses his position with the firm, he has a very good chance of getting another one because of the value he can bring to another firm. All he has to do is get visibility with other law firms and have a mastery of a script so that he clearly communicates his efficient and effective attributes. For instance, while the average lawyer generates 1,700 billable hours a year, he can average 1,870 billable hours per year, and did so in his prior position. If he gets out and works his network and tells this story effectively to enough people in the legal profession, he will get a job.

Whenever an employer hires someone, he or she must consider whether this job applicant will add value to the business. Every job applicant should consider this principle. Before you talk to a prospective employer, you should always ask yourself: What can I do for this company that will help it prosper? The answer had better include value above and beyond the cost of employing you.

Obviously, this is how law firms see it, and it's how every successful company looks at its workers. I used a law firm to illustrate because it is easy to see how the concept works using billable hours. Most positions have this dynamic going on, but often it is not as direct and visible as the billable-hours method is with the lawyers. Even if you are only being hired to sweep the floor, your work has value to the company that owns that floor. A clean workplace is safer, more efficient and more attractive to its customers, clients and other employees. *You should also know that someone somewhere in management is calculating the cost of your employment versus the value of your output.*

We all have some role in providing goods or services to others. That's why it's essential for each of us to understand how this work adds value to the businesses and institutions for which we work. If the company doesn't make money from your services, your employment with them won't last. When the economy is tight, this process usually plays out fast. I have worked in many corporate environments. The companies that succeed are always looking for greater efficiency, greater production and lower costs. In a successful company, efficient and productive employees will be hired and retained while others will be rejected or asked to leave.

"Value-added" in the workplace—tradesman

Here, we examine the importance of "value-added" by looking at a typical small business situation through the activities of an average plumber who makes customer service calls. While this is illustrated through a plumber, this example is similar to many other occupations including car mechanics, electricians, claims adjusters and technicians of all stripes.

Emma Lou is the sole proprietor of Emma Lou's Plumbing. Bubba is the one and only plumber in her employ. A full work year for Bubba consists of 2,080 hours (52 weeks x 40 hours a week). Bubba costs Emma Lou $25 per hour, or $52,000 per year. This includes all employee taxes and benefit expenses.

Emma Lou charges her customers $45 per service hour in addition to a $35 service charge for service calls. The service call is defined as a plumber showing up at a home or business. A service call in this scenario should take, on average, 30 minutes. An average workday should consist of six billed service hours and four service call charges. It's also extremely important that a plumber be courteous, not leave a mess and fix the problem without the need to go back. These activities are the plumber's expected output for an eight-hour workday. This results in receipts of $270 for the six service hours worked and $140 for the four service calls, for a total billing of $410 per day.

On an annual basis, this amounts to $70,200 billed for service hours worked and $36,400 billing for service calls, for total revenue of $106,600 per year. These numbers would be achieved only if Bubba is diligent and consistent throughout the year and delivers actual billable work equal to the 2,080 hours for which he is paid. An evaluation of these circumstances is a prime example of how a company looks at the productive output of its employees. In this example Bubba is paid for 2,080 hours, which should translate into $106,600 in billing revenue. That is the company's value expectation from employing Bubba; anything less is what's known as "not meeting expectations." This is an example of the value-added equation you should understand and strive to deliver.

Emma Lou pays Bubba $52,000 per year and generates $106,600 in customer billings from Bubba's work. This produces an after-labor net for Emma Lou of $54,600. From this, she must pay all her other business expenses with some left over to pay herself. In this example, her other expenses are $15,000, making her total expenses $67,000. So in this scenario, Bubba's "value-added" is the $39,600 Emma Lou gets to pay herself from profits realized from Bubba's work.

What happens to the business if Bubba leaves? That answer is easy: Emma Lou is effectively out of business because Bubba's billings are her entire revenue stream. Knowing that, do you think she might decide one day Bubba is too old and fire him? She might, but only if she has a death wish for her business. At a minimum, she must find a new plumber, a process that might cause an interruption in service to customers, reducing her profits.

What happens to her business if Bubba fails to do enough service calls to equal his $52,000 cost and cover the other business expenses of $15,000? At that point, Bubba's value to her falls dramatically. This is when she should give some thought to replacing him. If she doesn't, her business won't last very long.

What if one of Emma Lou's friends retires and closes her plumbing business and her outstanding employee, Earl Wayne, is put on the street with no job? His cost to his employer was $54,000, but Earl Wayne is extremely productive and is able to produce $125,000 in billing, nearly twice the rate of Bubba's current poor performance. Even if the economy is bad, do you think Earl Wayne will get a job? Absolutely. This guy is a moneymaker, and even in a tight job market, he will land on his feet. That's a very important secret most people don't seem to know. Good performers have better-than-average prospects of getting a job in bad times because the companies need them even more during tight economic times. Even if a company has no openings, they will be looking to rid themselves of low performers in favor of high performers. The high performer must, however, network well to make himself visible. As it happens, Earl Wayne asks his old boss to inquire of her business associates and friends to let them know about his (Earl Wayne's) availability and performance record.

Do you think Emma Lou will fire Bubba and hire Earl Wayne? I do, but only if Earl Wayne comes to the attention of Emma Lou—which he did as a result of the networking provided by his old boss. Do you think Emma Lou will spend a lot of time thinking about Earl Wayne's age, gender, body weight or politics, or do you think she will be more focused on his billing potential of $125,000? Yeah, me too; I think the focus will be exclusively on his billing potential.

While this may seem like a simplistic example, it is exactly how it happens in real life. In this example, the two men were evaluated by the dollar value of their respective service billings compared with the cost of their salary and related business expenses. You must examine your occupation and understand how you add value because it is exactly what employers evaluate when making hiring and firing decisions.

It will not be your age, gender, skin color or politics that gets you the job. It will be your perceived value to a prospective employer that will get you hired.

CHAPTER NINE

_____

Networking

Networking activities

Active networking is the best strategy for neutralizing the gatekeepers who throw away your résumés and applications. So, how many job-related appointments or events do you have scheduled for today? How many did you have last week?

People are a rich source of information, but they need to know specifically what you are interested in before they can share their knowledge and connections with you. Briefly and clearly tell them you are looking for information about job opportunities, introductions to people in your field of work, and help in positioning your résumé with the hiring authority.

Meeting face-to-face is essential. You use the Internet for research and most written communications, and the telephone for virtually all inquiries, follow-up and verbal communications. However, you cannot rely on these as your main methods of communication in making personal contact because nothing can be a substitute for face-to-face meetings. Remember from your own experience, it's much harder to blow someone off who's standing right in front of you.

Likewise, it is easier to establish a relationship in person. The primary goals of networking are: to gain an introduction to the hiring authority, to find where the jobs are and to get past the gatekeepers to position your résumé directly in front of the decision-maker. A majority of your time should revolve around quality networking activities. After all, networking can lead to face-to-face contact with people working in your target industry or with serious business people who may steer you to multiple opportunities.

Learn how to work a room and take advantage of every activity to meet people and engage them in a discussion about your profession. Ask them for contacts. Learn how to use the Internet to find business activities and opportunities. Once you have located activity related to your targeted industries, you can map out a strategy that puts you in proximity to the people involved. Arrange a schedule so you can make contact with them and ask questions. It helps to cultivate a relationship before soliciting much help. Don't be a pest, but show them you are curious, competent, interested and, most of all, very appreciative of their time.

A temp agency can be a terrific networking resource. The best agencies have important clients, and they strive to send them the best temps possible. If you present yourself well to these agencies, eventually you will earn their trust and be rewarded placements with their best clients. Research the agencies in your area and find the ones that handle jobs in your field. Approach these agencies as if they were your most important job opportunity. Always act and dress professionally, and make yourself available to most anything they offer you. The opportunities will get better as you prove yourself to them.

Illustration J-1.3 © *Edward H. Burrell*

Your networking will get you past the gatekeepers.

Be gently persistent

Job seekers often make requests or leave voice messages with their network contacts or referrals that go unanswered. This happens regularly for one of two reasons. First, the action is deliberate because the person has no intention of fulfilling the request. Second, it is unintended because the person got caught up in the hustle and bustle of their activities and forgot. Once forgotten the request or message fell out of sight and out of mind. In my experience, more often the reason is unintentional.

On many occasions I have been asked to call someone or return a call and frequently I failed to do so. Most of the time, I had every intention of making the call, but simply got distracted and forgot. Recently, a very good friend asked me for some business information that was important for him to have. I had the information, I wanted him to have it and I fully intended to give it to him. Three weeks later, I happened to see him at an event we both attended. The minute I saw him I remembered what I had forgotten. I was horrified and as soon as I got home I rounded up the information and sent it to him.

Don't give up, get mad or write the person off, rather recognize your requests are competing against a swirl of other activities and will often lose visibility. To help minimize this fate, you must find ways to convey gentle reminders to those you have called or solicited for assistance. If the request was ignored because of reason number one, your reminders will be for naught, but if it was because of reason number two, you will likely get a quick response. Be gently persistent.

How to find networking contacts

First, it is wise to create a narrative that fits your circumstances and personality. In other words, prepare what you are planning to say to the people with whom you network. This is where you use your professional narratives. Develop an introduction to go with your narrative and practice talking until you are totally comfortable discussing it with anyone. It is easy to ask a question when joining a group, so start there and your conversations will become easier with practice and repetition.

You are looking for people who work in your profession, industry or companies that you are targeting for employment. Remember your goal is face-to-face contact with five to eight people in positions related to your industry every day. Anyone who works for a big, viable corporation of any kind might provide you with leads you never considered. To get started building your network, begin with the people you know—friends, family, people you have worked with previously, classmates, neighbors and people in any organization with which you are affiliated. Many churches have programs for those looking for work. Seek leads from all of these sources and ask for an introduction to the people they recommend you contact. If they can't help you directly, ask them if they know where there is activity in your profession or if they can give you a lead in one of the companies you have interest. As I mentioned above, temporary agencies already have the contacts you need; all you have to do is prove yourself to these agencies through your performance during your job assignments and they will gladly send you to their best clients. Follow up with everyone. You never know who will give you the connection you need to land that perfect job.

Employment agencies (a.k.a. head hunters)

While some agencies do both permanent and temporary placements, in this section I am focused on the permanent placement aspect of the employment firm's business. People often ask if they are expected to pay a fee to the agency for a job placement. The answer is "no." The fees are paid by the company doing the hiring, unless you are tangled up with a scam of some sort. It's possible to have circumstances where a legitimate company collects a modest fee from job seekers, but this is not the norm. If faced with this circumstance, you want to proceed with extreme caution because there are charlatans willing to take advantage of desperate job seekers who don't read the fine print. Some will charge a fee up front and simply provide you with worthless job leads.

On the other hand, legitimate employment agencies are a terrific source for job opportunities. The agencies vary in their business model—some specialize in the recruitment of CEOs, others specialize in medical doctors or senior executives of all sorts. Some focus on professions like computer system technology, engineering and accounting. Others are generalists that work with pretty much everything else. Seek out the permanent placement agencies that handle your occupation, and let them help you find your best corporate opportunity.

CHAPTER TEN

The interview process

Getting a job offer is similar to making a sale, only in this situation you are selling yourself. You might be the best technician in the world, but if you can't communicate effectively the attributes, skills and experience that make you great, you won't make the sale.

Interview preparations

Always put your best foot forward, but don't stretch the truth or try to appear more knowledgeable than you are. Experienced interviewers are trained to detect inconsistencies and fabrications. Usually, there is no perfect candidate. Consequently, they are not expecting a perfect fit, so all you need to do is match up well. If the interviewer knows, or even senses, you are making stuff up, you are finished. With that in mind, it is perfectly acceptable to tailor your résumé and interview preparation to the specific job and company. You want to emphasize those parts of your background that qualify you for the position. As long as you are properly prepared, you will come across as relaxed and confident.

Illustration J-14 © *Edward H. Burrell*

Don't stretch your answers or résumé to try to be a perfect fit

Determine 90 percent of the questions in advance

It is critical to give serious thought and analysis to the subject matter of your interview before you step foot in the interview. While you may not identify the exact questions asked during your interviews, you will cover the subject matter from which the questions are drawn and should easily adapt your responses. The sources of 90 percent of the interview questions are as follows:

- 70 percent of the questions will be associated with:
  ° The functions of the job
  ° The activities associated with these functions

- 10 percent will be:
  ° Questions directly related to your résumé.
- 10 percent taken:
  ° From a list of "the most commonly asked interview questions."

1) The 70 percent or so of the questions asked are pertinent to the target job, and to common circumstances that occur in that job environment. Every job is made up of functional components. Questions will be related to the functions of the specific job and from activities associated with these functions. It is important to analyze your job or profession through to its component activities. Next, think through the best way to accomplish each of these activities. Recount all the tasks required in a detailed written outline. Create a two-minute discussion on each function or step that makes up your job, and practice talking about them.

2) Your résumé or job application will generate specific follow-up questions. Typically, this will be **10 percent** of the questions asked, but could be more depending on how much intrigue is created by your résumé. You can expect to be asked questions related to your past jobs and more direct questions on any perceived deficiencies in your work history or career. Be familiar with your résumé and be prepared to answer questions about it. Give results-oriented answers where possible. Be prepared to give well-thought-out answers to questions about your résumé weaknesses and employment gaps, and especially prepare for the questions you hope they never ask.

3) You can expect some of the so-called "most commonly asked interview questions" or variations thereof to be **at least another 10 percent** of the questions you will answer. You can snoop around the Internet and find the latest version for your area. You will recognize them easily, and below I have listed several:

- Tell us about yourself?
- Why should we hire you?
- Where do you see yourself in five years?
- What are some of your strengths?
- What are some of your hobbies?
- How do you evaluate success?
- Describe a difficult work situation and how you overcame it?
- What did you like or dislike about your previous job?
- What do you expect from a supervisor?
- Describe your work style?
- What is good customer service?

✳ ✳ ✳

If you really want to shine during your interviews, you should learn how to relate the functions of the job logically and comprehensively. That means that before you go in for the interview, you should fully examine why this position exists, what the most important functions are, how they work, and what the goals are. If the job entails recurring activities—such as managing inventories, hiring and managing seasonal workers, or examining and evaluating products and markets—be ready to describe these work cycles and the role this job plays in them. Your knowledge and understanding of the big picture will help you perform and make you shine during your interviews.

Four of the most dreaded questions

We all have questions we hope to avoid, yet those are the first ones for which you should prepare. There are two reasons for doing so. First, you are going to be asked difficult questions and they require well-thought-out answers. As you can well imagine, thoughtful answers are best formulated in advance. Second, just sitting there during the interview worrying about the dreaded questions to come will cause you to lack confidence and will hurt your overall interview performance.

The questions you don't prepare for will be more difficult than need be. Identify all the questions you expect to face, dreaded or otherwise, and write out your responses. Practice giving your answers to an audience of the toughest characters you can find. Once you are confident and comfortable with that crowd, you will be ready.

Below, I have listed the most common "dreaded questions" along with some sample explanations and thoughts on how best to answer them. Tell the truth and take responsibility where appropriate, but always keep the story line positive. Don't belabor the point; rather, keep your answers short and concise. The key message is to prepare for the dreaded questions. This exercise will increase your confidence.

1. Why did you get fired from your last job?

If you were let go because the company downsized or moved to another location, then simply state the facts of the situation. On the other hand, if you were let go because of performance issues, I suggest you craft a truthful answer using a format similar to mine below. Make it clear you learned from the experience, accept responsibility and remain positive.

"I desperately needed a job and made a mistake by jumping at the first opportunity. The position was not a good fit for me and I did not perform anywhere near my ability. My job search is much more targeted now and that has led me to this company, where I think I can make a significant contribution."

2. Please explain the gaps in your employment history?

When I look at a résumé, I expect the person to account for all their time since graduation. However, when I evaluate a candidate's résumé, I focus in detail only on the last ten years or so. This is not an endorsement of a four-page résumé; instead it is a call for brevity. It is easy to do. I have a three sentence paragraph that describes 10 years of long-ago military service that covers four assignments in three different states. It is best to condense and summarize your early work history.

If there are years missing or unaccounted for in your employment history, employers naturally think you may be hiding something. They will imagine all sorts of negative scenarios. You don't want people's imaginations to run wild, so don't leave physical gaps in your employment history. You may not have had a full-time job, but that doesn't mean you weren't constructively engaged in alternate activities. Listed below are examples of the activities to which I refer.

For those who have been out of the workforce due to family considerations such as care giving for elderly parents or stay-at-home mothers, simply list your activity as you would any other job. Explain the scope of your responsibilities and what you accomplished. List the dates as you would any other job.

If you worked at a temporary job or several temp jobs while looking for permanent employment, you have an easy story to tell. Simply make one entry for that time period. Your narrative is: "Worked a number of temporary jobs ranging from stocking shelves to waiting tables while seeking permanent employment."

Many people have periods of unemployment with no real alternative activity to offer. They were out of a job and looking for another. The longer the time the harder it is to explain. I suggest you create a chronology of the self-improvement and job-seeking activities in which you have engaged. Rehearse your explanation to make your best case in explaining what you've done to keep your skills current and to find a job.

Answering employment history questions during an interview will be a whole lot easier if you don't leave unexplained gaps. Rather, fill in the alternate activities and frame the information in your résumé similar to my examples above. Use your own circumstances; mine are just meant to be examples. This will minimize the number of questions and make it easier to answer the questions you're asked.

3. What is your major weakness?

Make sure you know this question is directed at your professional life with regard to your job skills and not your personal life. I say this because I have heard some astounding confessions during interviews in which I have participated as an interviewer.

I find this question the most difficult to answer because during an interview I am there to sell myself and to do otherwise just feels so wrong. I suggest you play it safe and pick universal issues with which we all struggle. For example, we all have to learn how to set priorities and manage our time. So, talk about shortcomings like those and accentuate the steps you have taken to improve.

4. What are your salary requirements?

Before you start talking salary with a prospective employer you should do some homework and determine what the salary range is for the position you seek. You can find salary information by searching the Internet. Once you find market value information for the position, you can respond to this question by citing the salary range and explaining where you see yourself in that range. Be prepared to back that up with examples of what you have done to merit the level of pay you request. You can also state that you don't want salary issues to get in the way of you getting the job, and indicate you have some flexibility.

Prior to scheduling an interview, the Human Resources (HR) department or a recruiter will often clarify with you what the salary range is for the job. They may ask you what your salary requirements are before they tell you anything. If you have this conversation with HR, I think you're done talking salary until the company makes you a job offer. Under no circumstances would I recommend you bring up salary issues during the actual interview process. Let them make an offer first, and then, if you aren't satisfied, try to negotiate a better deal. Be courteous and professional, and make sure you thank them for the offer. Remain very diplomatic as you do your best to convince them why they should increase their offer. Keep in mind the company may have budget constraints or policies they must honor.

Preparations needed for behavioral interviews

Many traditional interview questions are easy to prepare for, so, it is difficult for the interviewer to gauge the true skill level of the candidate. From the responses given by the candidate, the interviewer tries to discern if this candidate is the real deal or just someone really well rehearsed in answering the likely questions.

As a consequence of this dilemma, many businesses have moved to a questioning technique known as behavioral questions. In short, these questions require you to give specific examples of what you did in certain work-related situations. You may be asked to explain a whole range of actions associated with these situations including: what you said, what you did, what you thought, how you reacted, what you learned, what you would do differently and what you did as follow-up actions. These types of questions make it easy for the interviewer to ask very specific and pointed follow-up questions. Upon further questioning, if you were making up your scenarios, your stories will likely start to unravel.

There are seemingly endless variations in the behavioral questions that can be asked, but I have noticed a common theme to the questions. The behavioral questions seem to revolve around certain skills and temperaments. I have zeroed in on those most important and common in the list below.

To prepare for a tough behavioral interview, take yourself back to your previous workplace and think through how you handled situations that required you to demonstrate the following skills and attributes:

- Problem-solving skills
- Leadership abilities
- Team player qualities
- Flexibility
- Decision-making abilities
- Conflict resolution skills
- People skills
- Ability to make and set priorities
- Attitude
- Ingenuity
- Performance under stress or adversity
- Critical-thinking skills

If you fail to take the time to think through these scenarios in advance of your behavioral interviews, you're in for a very painful experience. People unprepared for situational questions typically remember half the story line and end up delivering a very poor presentation of how they handled the situations.

✳　　✳　　✳

Considerations during your interviews

- Smile, and greet your interviewer(s) with a firm handshake (meet them as friends, not enemies).
- Thank them for the opportunity to meet with them.
- Dress professionally with your best business clothes.
- Sit up straight and keep your hands away from your face.
- Don't look around. Look the person in the eyes when talking to them.
- Don't apologize for anything. Rather, offer to follow up with additional material.
- Don't be defensive.
- Relax, but show interest and passion for the position.
- Listen carefully to the interviewers and learn from what they say. Make sure you answer the exact questions they ask and seek clarification for questions you don't understand.
- If you don't know the answer to a particular question, tell them you don't know.
- Questions are designed to hear you talk. Give brief, crisp answers, stay on topic and don't generalize.
- Don't make negative comments about your previous supervisor or company. You cannot make that sound good, no matter what you think.
- Don't wish the interview was over. See the interview as an opportunity to talk about your next job with your potential new employer and colleagues.
- At the end of the interview, express an interest in the job and ask them if they have a timeline for completion of this hiring action.

Interviewer's considerations

- Does this candidate have the job experience necessary to handle this job?
- Does this candidate have meaningful accomplishments that prepare him or her for the target job?
- Does this candidate have a mastery of the functions of the job?
- Does this candidate have the right attitude, communication skills, and likability?
- Can this candidate learn the job, become proficient, and give us a fair day's work?
- Does this person bring value and will he or she move the needle and make things better?
- Do I want to be around this person every day and will he or she get along with others?
- Has this person been successful in a similar environment?
- Will this person show up every day and on time?
- Does this person have potential?
- Will this person steal from or embarrass the company?
- If difficulties arise, will this person act honorably, or will he or she evade responsibility and exploit the situation through threats or lawsuits?

Actions behind the interview curtain

- Even in good times, some jobs generate hundreds of résumés.
- The first pass through a pile of résumés screens for the easy rejects. Résumés are often sorted by the gatekeepers—drones assigned to match the résumés against a template of requirements. If the résumés are in an electronic format, then this elimination sort is done with a word search software program. Before you submit your résumé, check to make sure it emphasizes

your qualifications for this particular job. Read the job description with special attention to the skills and experience requirements.

- The hiring process is a lot of work and a distraction to the business. People are anxious, even excited, about finding the right person, but often dread going through the process.
- HR staff will often conduct preliminary interviews to create a pool of qualified candidates.
- The real interview is usually conducted by the person under whom you will work.
- The higher positions will often be interviewed by a team of people who will select a slate of candidates for final interview by the hiring authority.

Anytime you can bypass screening and preliminary interviews and go straight to the hiring authority, you dramatically increase your chances. In most instances, just knowing someone will not get you the job, but it will often get you an interview. Find contacts capable of steering your résumé to the hiring manager at companies where you are applying. This is why I stress the importance of networking.

Job candidates should know

- Arrive a little early and relax.
- Even though the economy is tight, 90 out of 100 people have jobs.
- The company needs you. Don't give them a reason to think otherwise.
- Attitude means a lot. Be positive, upbeat and energetic.
- When in doubt, tell the truth. Tell it the rest of the time too.

- Quality interviews are hard to come by, so it is important to give your best effort at each opportunity.
- Know what value you bring to a prospective employer.
- Likability takes place in the first 30 to 90 seconds.
- Interview questions are always answered. By that I mean I have never heard of a job applicant who refused to answer a question, so prepare accordingly.

It's been said that it takes three days to prepare a good, off-the-cuff 10-minute speech. You are preparing something like that here, so perfect the process of talking about the functions of your profession, what you did and what you can do. When preparing for an interview, keep in mind you will be expected to talk for at least 45 minutes, not 10 minutes. This will also be especially valuable for your networking activities. If you appear to be a high-quality professional with a good grasp of your profession, people will refer you to their friends and contacts to help them in conjunction with helping you. You benefit, but their true motivation is to help their business associates and friends because they believe in you, and this adds enormous power to their referral.

CHAPTER ELEVEN

—————

Post interview activities

What determines who gets the job offer?

In my experience, conducting several hundred job interviews, job placements are determined as a result of an applicant's performance during the interview. Although many people choose to believe otherwise, I've never heard anyone say: This person is perfect for the job, but is too old, too young, or of the wrong gender, ethnicity, politics, religion, etc. Rather, most discussions revolve around whether the person is a good fit for the position, or which person is the best fit for the position. "Fit" summarized is: Your accomplishments in the sequence of jobs that prepared you for the target job; your mastery of the job's functions; and your attitude, attributes, communication skills, likability and perceived potential.

Many people choose to believe they didn't get the job because they were treated unfairly or because of some unjust attitude or policy. Or, they state the famous response, "They gave it to an internal candidate." It's a lot easier to believe you didn't get the job because somehow the deck was stacked against you than to believe you didn't compete well for the job. The problem with this line of reasoning is that if you let yourself off the hook and falsely place the blame, you will have no chance of correcting what issues really need improvement.

This is not to say that someone over 50 can't give a bad impression by seeming tired, too old to learn or set in one's ways. Those of you advanced in years can't drag yourselves into the interview room yawning and fluffing up a pillow. Everyone needs to show energy and passion. Especially those over 50.

Follow-up

It is essential that you make contact after an interview, so ask the interviewer when would be a good time to follow up about the opportunity. Even if you forget to ask, or do not get a specific answer, go ahead and follow up after a day or two. Your follow-up should include a thank you note and an expression of interest in the company. You should follow this same process when you make in-person inquiries with hiring managers or key players in any company. While I love e-mail, you will be far more effective if you follow up with a handwritten personal note.

Don't

There will be occasions during your job search when a specific job will look promising, or you will get words of encouragement with a promise of a callback or second interview. Do not become paralyzed by the expectation of this one callback and stop your job search activities. From my observations, a majority of the time you will not hear from them again. The waiting and excessive anticipation will hurt your psyche. You need many good leads before a tangible job offer comes about, so don't lose your momentum.

Illustration J-1.5 © *Edward H. Burrell*

Do not become paralyzed by the expectation of this one callback.

CHAPTER TWELVE

Summary

Getting a job is a lot like making a sale. Your product might be the best in the world, but if you can't present it well you won't make the sale. So prepare the product (you) by developing the attributes of a highly desirable job applicant: Present a neat appearance, exhibit a positive attitude, demonstrate passion, exude energy, display confidence, express value awareness, convey competence and exemplify an unequivocal mastery of your profession.

Job plan strategies

Futurists predict, on average, a person entering the work force will change jobs 10 times before they reach the age of 40. So, it's not all about finding a job. Rather, it's about developing the ability to find your next 10 jobs. You are hired by getting interviews and doing well when interviewed. You get interviews by getting up early and working a plan that gets you out of the house and face to face with five to eight people related to your industry every day. Study the functions of your profession, then practice talking about how efficiently you can accomplish its tasks. Make it clear how you will add value to their company, and you will do well in your interviews. Finding a job is about making its pursuit the highest priority in your life. So turn off the television and make a resolution to not turn it back on until you have a job.

Résumé tactics

No matter what format you use, remember the top half of the first page of your résumé is the most critical. Make sure you communicate clearly what you've done on the top half of page one. When describing your prior job responsibilities on your résumé, be sure to explain the significant contributions you made to your previous employers. In all cases, after you describe the job, you should explain what you did, the contributions you made, and more specifically, how you moved the needle and made things better.

Master your profession

It is important to analyze your profession through to a detailed breakdown of its component activities and then recount them in a detailed written outline. Create a two-minute discussion on each function or step and practice talking about how best to accomplish the tasks from your own experience. Think about situations that commonly occur in that job environment. You should also be able to identify and recite things that commonly go wrong and what must be done to accomplish these functions in the best way possible. Be conversant between the best way and the wrong way to accomplish each task.

Know your "value-added equation"

"Value-added" is the notion that an employee should earn his or her company the amount the employee is being paid, plus additional money to help cover a share of all the costs of doing business, plus something more. The "something more" is profit. Profits add value to a business, and that is the employer's ultimate goal when hiring any employee. In most occupations, if you are not working efficiently and effectively, you will soon be out of a job, and you will find it difficult to get another one. This is true because companies do not want to hire inefficient and ineffective employees. *You should also know that someone somewhere in management is calculating the cost of your employment versus the value of your output.*

Your networking campaign

Once you have mastered communicating a solid grasp of your profession, you appear to others as a high-quality professional. This will motivate the people you meet to refer you to their business contacts. They will do it to help their friends and business associates in conjunction with helping you. This adds enormous power to their referral. Any time you can bypass the gatekeepers and go straight to the hiring authority, you dramatically increase your chances of being offered the job. Remember your goal is face-to-face contact with five to eight people in positions related to your industry every day. Find contacts capable of steering your résumé to the hiring manager at companies where you are applying. This is what I mean by networking.

Prepare for the interview

Displaying confidence and competence during your interviews is impressive and attractive to your prospective employer. While you can't fake confidence or competence, you can take steps to create both. Use the methods identified in this book to determine 90 percent of the interview questions likely to be asked in advance of the interview. It's more than just knowing the questions. You must communicate the answers well. So, practice your answers. Stay on point, be concise and don't generalize. Comprehensive preparation is the key. Before you sit down in the interview chair, you should be clear on how you can help a prospective employer. If you don't understand how you can add value, you need to figure it out quickly.

Interview performance considerations

Most job placements are determined as a result of an applicant's performance during the interview. Likability takes place in the first 30 to 90 seconds. Smile and greet your interviewer(s) with a firm handshake (meet them as friends, not enemies). Don't wish the interview was over. Rather, see the interview as an opportunity to talk about your next job with your potential new employer and colleagues.

✳   ✳   ✳

Gain a mastery of these concepts and you will get interviews and do well when interviewed. As a consequence of your strong interview performance, you will be offered employment opportunities.

www.ingramcontent.com/pod-product-compliance
Lightning Source LLC
Chambersburg PA
CBHW022341280326
41934CB00006B/734